WEATHER

First published in the UK in 2019 by

Ivy Kids

An imprint of The Quarto Group
The Old Brewery
6 Blundell Street
London N7 9BH
United Kingdom
www.QuartoKnows.com

A CIP record for this book is available from the Library of Congress.

ISBN: 978-1-78240-912-0

This book was conceived, designed & produced by

Ivy Kids

58 West Street, Brighton BN1 2RA, United Kingdom

PUBLISHER Susan Kelly
MANAGING EDITOR Susie Behar
ART DIRECTOR Hanri van Wyk
DESIGNER Kevin Knight
IN-HOUSE DESIGNER Kate Haynes
IN-HOUSE EDITORS Lucy Menzies &
Hannah Dove

Manufactured in Guangdong, China TT052019

1 3 5 7 9 10 8 6 4 2

My FIRST Fact File

WEATHER

EVERYTHING you NEED to KNOW

BY DR. JEN GREEN   ILLUSTRATED BY TOM WOOLLEY
CONSULTANT: PROF. ADAM SCAIFE

IVY KIDS

CONTENTS

EVERYTHING you NEED to KNOW

INTRODUCTION

Before you begin this book, check what is happening outdoors. Is the air warm, hot, or freezing? Is it calm or breezy? It may be sunny or cloudy, or perhaps rain, sleet, or snow is falling. All these conditions are the weather—the state of the air at a particular place and time.

In some parts of the world, the weather stays the same for days or even weeks. But in many places, it changes constantly, as storm clouds move in to cover a blue sky, or the sun peeps through after rain. Ever-changing weather keeps us guessing, and even the climate, which is the general weather for a region measured over many years, is changing.

Weather affects each and every one of us every day. It affects where we live and how we travel, the clothes we wear, and what we do. We also rely on the weather to grow our food. This book will explore the many types of weather and climate. It will explain the awesome forces behind weather systems, and describe all the different sorts of weather that affect us around the globe.

Think about the last time you saw a rainbow. Did you know that a rainbow happens when sunlight shines through raindrops?

THE SUN

The Sun is the nearest star to Earth, at a distance of 93 million miles. Even though it's so far away from us, the heat and light energy created by the Sun travels though space and reaches our planet. Imagine how hot it must be! It's this heat and light energy that gives us weather. As Earth orbits the Sun (moves around it on a set path), our weather and seasons change.

QUICK FACTS

The Sun creates heat and light energy. This energy gives us weather on Earth.

SOLAR ENERGY

Heat and light energy from the Sun can be turned into other kinds of energy. A device called a solar panel catches the Sun's rays and turns them into electricity. We can use the electricity made by solar panels to power our homes.

SOLAR PANEL

The Sun heats Earth most at the Equator
(an imaginary line around the center
of Earth) and least at the Poles.

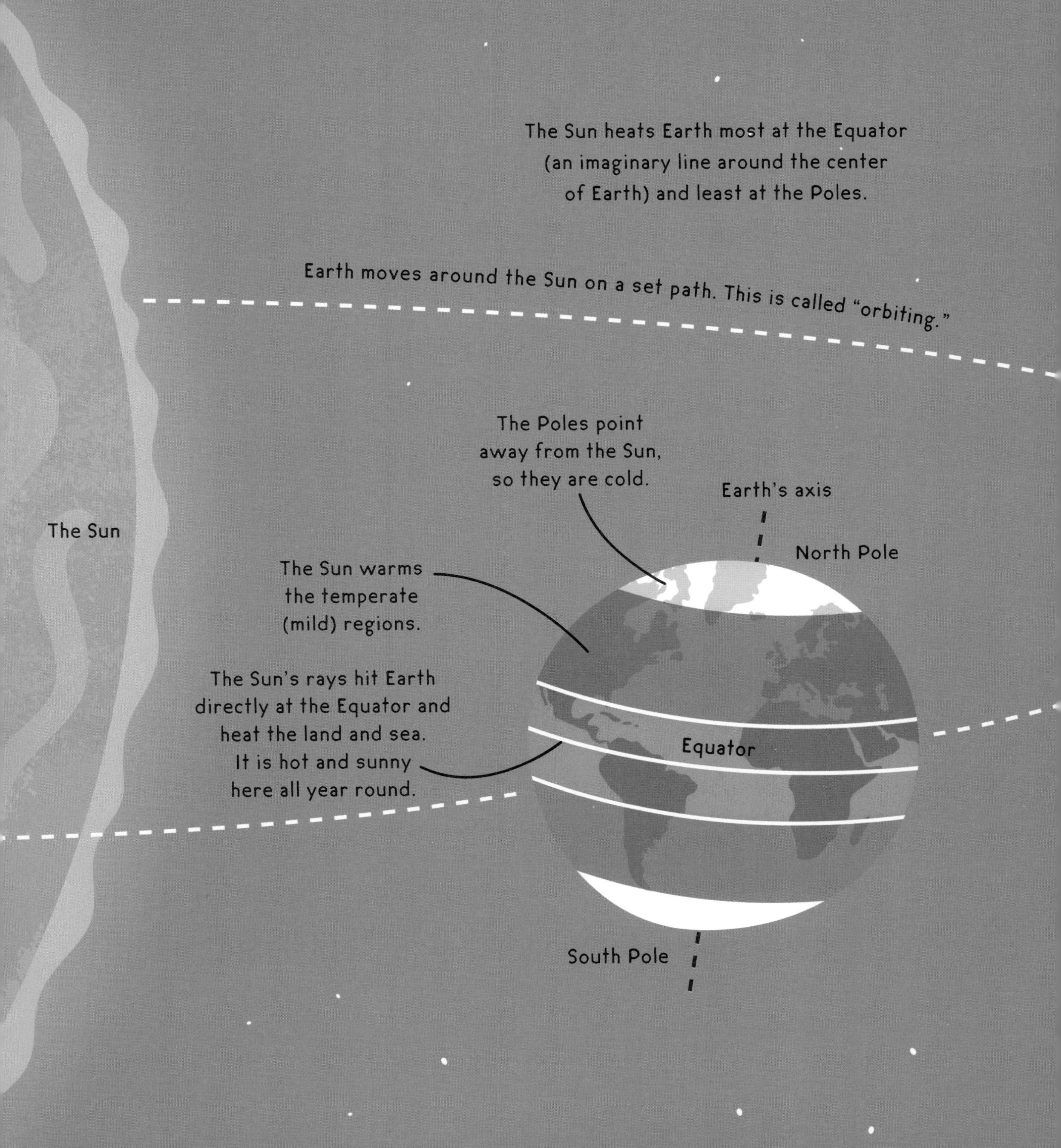

Earth moves around the Sun on a set path. This is called "orbiting."

The Poles point
away from the Sun,
so they are cold.

Earth's axis

The Sun

North Pole

The Sun warms
the temperate
(mild) regions.

The Sun's rays hit Earth
directly at the Equator and
heat the land and sea.
It is hot and sunny
here all year round.

Equator

South Pole

THE ATMOSPHERE

Surrounding our planet is a blanket of gases called the atmosphere. These gases protect Earth from the Sun's heat, making conditions that we can live in. The atmosphere absorbs heat from the Sun and reacts with it in different ways, creating different kinds of weather. The atmosphere is mostly made up of just two gases: nitrogen and oxygen (the gas that we need to live). The weight of the atmosphere pushing down on Earth creates a force called air pressure.

TEST AIR PRESSURE

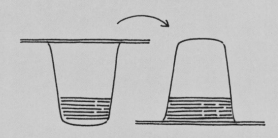

You need:

A cup full of water

A piece of card

An adult helper

1. Cover the cup with the card.
2. Take the cup to a sink and turn it upside down, holding the piece of card firmly against the cup.
3. Take your hand away from the card — the water stays in the upside-down cup! The air pressure is greater outside the cup than inside it, and this prevents the water from pouring out.

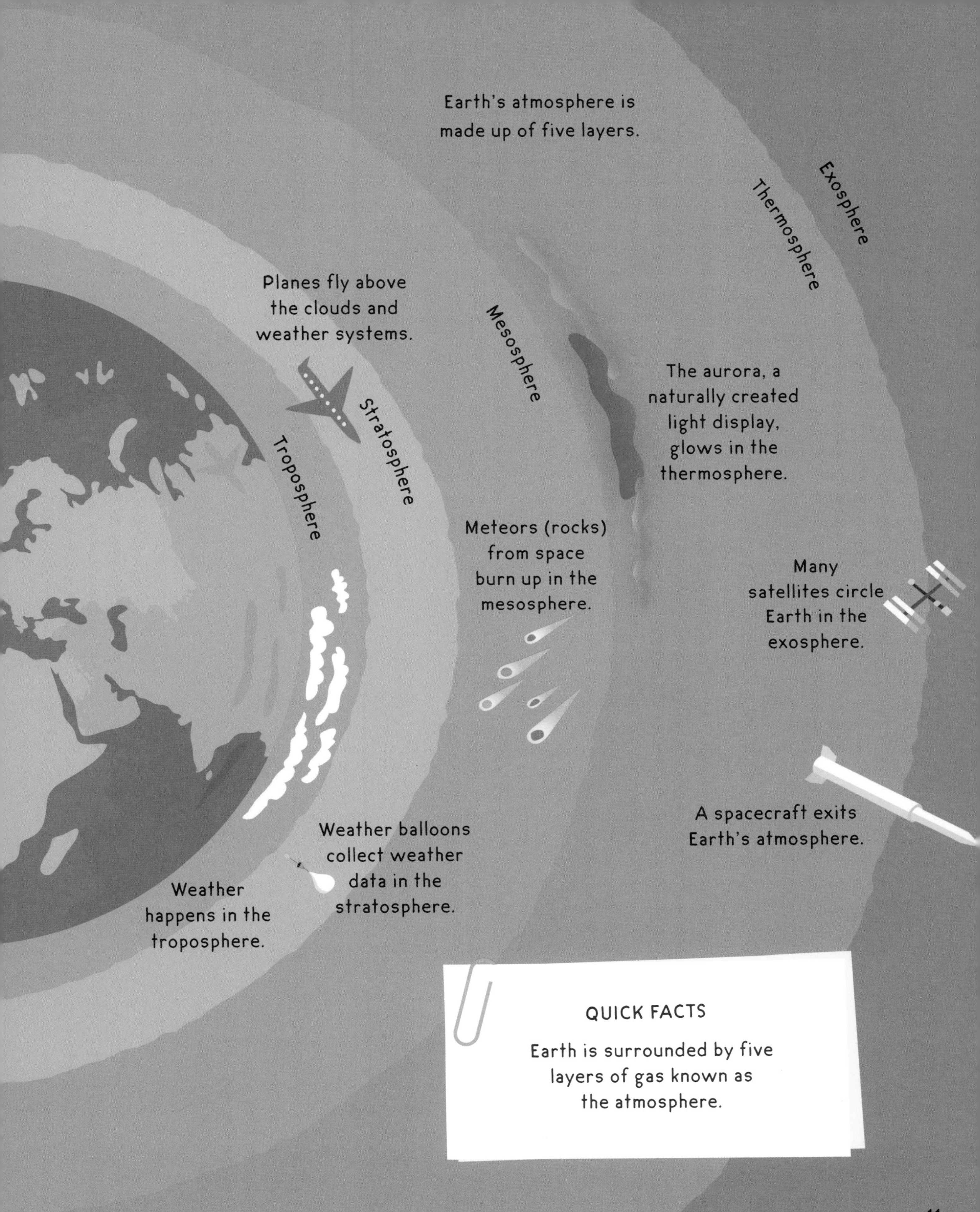

Earth's atmosphere is made up of five layers.

Exosphere

Thermosphere

Mesosphere

Stratosphere

Troposphere

Planes fly above the clouds and weather systems.

The aurora, a naturally created light display, glows in the thermosphere.

Meteors (rocks) from space burn up in the mesosphere.

Many satellites circle Earth in the exosphere.

A spacecraft exits Earth's atmosphere.

Weather balloons collect weather data in the stratosphere.

Weather happens in the troposphere.

QUICK FACTS

Earth is surrounded by five layers of gas known as the atmosphere.

OCEANS AND SEAS

We live on a watery planet—more than two-thirds of Earth's surface is covered by oceans and seas! This has a big effect on the world's weather. Oceans and seas store heat energy from the Sun. The water is constantly being stirred by winds, waves, tides, and currents (the movement of water in the ocean in a particular direction). These help to spread the Sun's heat around Earth.

The currents flow around in huge circles called gyres.

The shape of continents influences the gyres.

Warm and cold currents of water flow around the world, affecting the weather.

Water that flows from polar seas toward the Equator cools the lands it flows past.

Tropical currents move warm water toward the Poles, heating the landmasses they flow past.

POLAR SEAS

Polar seas are cold and mostly ice-covered where the Sun's rays are less strong. Animals here have adapted to the freezing conditions. Polar bears have thick fur to keep them warm, even on the bottom of their paws. They also have big feet for walking on snow and swimming through icy water. Their white coat stops them being seen by the animals they hunt.

QUICK FACTS

Earth's oceans help to spread heat from the Sun around the globe.

WINDS

Wind is air on the move. From a gentle breeze to a howling gale, all winds are caused by one thing — differences in air pressure. Air pressure is the weight of the air in the atmosphere and it can change with altitude (height) and temperature. Heat energy from the Sun is absorbed by the ocean or land, warming the air above it. Warm air is lighter than cold air, so it rises. Cooler air rushes into the space where air has risen. The movement of air at different pressures produces wind.

QUICK FACTS

Winds are currents of moving air that can be measured in strength and direction.

COMPARE WIND SPEEDS

You need:

A toy windmill

A marker pen

A timer

Compare wind speeds with a simple toy windmill on a stick.

1. Mark one sail with a marker pen.
2. On a day with light wind, hold the windmill into the wind. Use the timer to count how many times the marked sail passes the stick in a minute.
3. Try it another day when you think it's breezier.

The Beaufort Scale measures wind
strengths, ranging from dead calm
at 0 to a raging hurricane at 12.

0 Calm
Wind speed: Less than 1 mph

Ocean is flat like a mirror

3 Gentle breeze
Wind speed: 8 — 12 mph

Small waves — crests begin to form

5 Fresh breeze
Wind speed: 19 — 24 mph

Moderate waves — small trees sway

7 Near gale
Wind speed: 32 — 38 mph

Ocean heaps up — large trees bend

10 Storm
Wind speed: 55 — 63 mph

Very high waves — trees are uprooted

12 Hurricane
Wind speed: 73 mph or higher

Violent waves and destruction

CLIMATE

What's the difference between weather and climate? Weather is whatever is happening in the air at any particular moment—it could be raining or snowing. Climate is the bigger picture—the regular pattern of weather over many years. Three main factors affect a region's climate: distance from the Equator (latitude), height of the land (altitude), and distance from the sea.

The snowy peak has a polar climate.

Upper slopes have a cool temperate climate, with coniferous trees.

Lower slopes have a warm temperate climate, with deciduous trees.

The rain forest has a tropical climate.

Polar climate

Temperate climate

Tropical climate

Temperate climate

Polar climate

Sun's rays

Polar climates and mountain climates are very cold. Tropical climates are very hot. A temperate climate is in between.

The ocean keeps the coast cool in summer and warm in winter.

ADAPTING TO CLIMATE

Animals that live in very hot places adapt to their environments. For example, the fennec fox, an animal that lives in hot climates, has thick, sand-colored fur that keeps it warm in the cold desert at night. This fur also reflects sunlight to keep it cool during the day and helps to camouflage it in the desert.

QUICK FACTS

Climate is the usual pattern of weather in a region.

BIOMES

Different plants have adapted to different climates. Spiky cacti grow well in a desert, but you won't see them in a rain forest. In the same way, rain forest trees such as mahogany would die in a desert. Varying climates all over Earth create huge habitats called biomes. Each biome has its own types of plants, such as grass or coniferous trees.

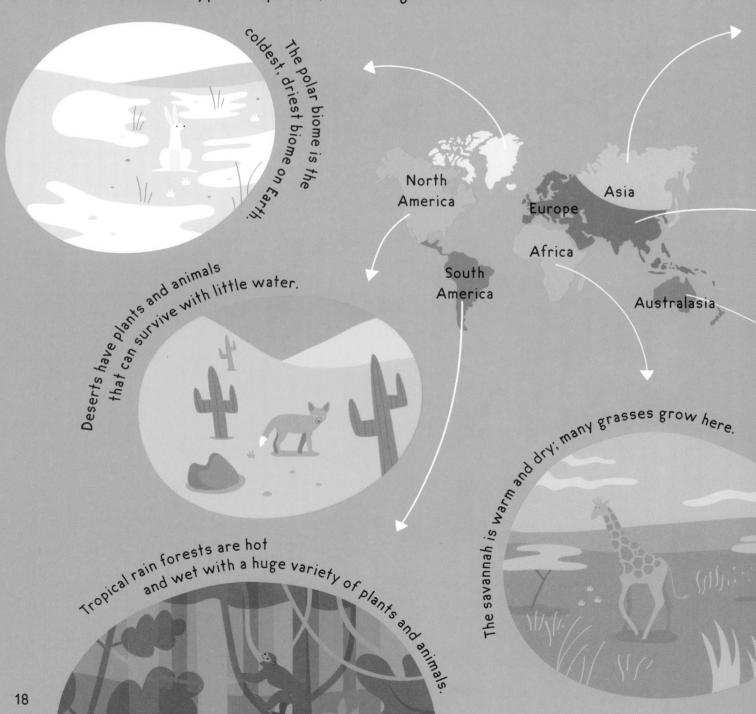

The polar biome is the coldest, driest biome on Earth.

Deserts have plants and animals that can survive with little water.

Tropical rain forests are hot and wet with a huge variety of plants and animals.

The savannah is warm and dry; many grasses grow here.

North America

South America

Europe

Africa

Asia

Australasia

The world's various climates create different biomes. Here are some examples.

The taiga has short summers and coniferous trees.

Temperate regions have deciduous forests.

The interior of Australia is dry scrubland called the Outback.

WHICH ANIMALS?

Different climates suit different kinds of animals. Can you match each animal with the biome it lives in?

Arctic fox	desert
jaguar	savannah
zebra	polar
camel	rain forest

See page 48 for the answer

QUICK FACTS

Biomes are large areas of Earth with a particular climate, and animals and plants that have adapted to live there.

SEASONS

Seasons happen because Earth tilts on its axis— an imaginary line through the North and South Poles — as it circles the Sun. Earth is always tilted in the same direction. The Equator divides Earth into a top half and a bottom half— the Northern and Southern Hemispheres. When it's summer in one hemisphere, it's winter in the other because of Earth's tilt.

QUICK FACTS

The seasons change on Earth according to how the planet tilts toward or away from the Sun.

SHOW THE SEASONS

You need:

An apple with a stalk

A dark room with a lamp in the middle

1. Imagine the stalk is the North Pole and the other end the South Pole. Tilt the North Pole toward the lamp (the Sun). It's summer in the Northern Hemisphere.
2. Keeping Earth tilted at the same angle in the same direction, move it to the other side of the Sun. Now the Southern Hemisphere has summer!

As Earth orbits the Sun, the Northern and Southern Hemispheres have different seasons.

Earth's axis

In December, it's summer in the Southern Hemisphere because it's tilted toward the Sun.

In March, the Southern Hemisphere has fall while it's spring in the Northern Hemisphere.

In June, it's summer in the Northern Hemisphere because it's tilted toward the Sun.

In September, it's spring in the Southern Hemisphere, and in the Northern Hemisphere, it's fall.

WATER CYCLE

Did you know that moisture moves constantly between the land, the air, and the oceans? This is called the water cycle. It means that the water that runs out of your tap was once in the clouds, in the ocean, and in rivers or lakes.

Warm air rises and cools. The moisture condenses (turns back into water) and forms clouds.

The Sun's warmth makes water from oceans and lakes evaporate into the air (become a gas called water vapor).

QUICK FACTS

Water flows around Earth in the water cycle.

Most of the rainwater drains into lakes and rivers and returns to the ocean.

Water evaporates into the air to form clouds as it warms, and condenses and falls back to Earth as rain as it cools.

MAKE A WATER CYCLE

Rain falls from the clouds.

Some rainwater soaks into the ground.

You need:

A jug of water

A large bowl

A small glass

Plastic wrap

A pebble

An adult helper

1. Pour some water into the bowl and put the empty glass in the middle.

2. Cover the bowl tightly with plastic wrap and place the pebble on top.

3. Put the bowl on a sunny windowsill for a few days. There should be water in the glass! The Sun evaporated the water, which condensed onto the plastic wrap and fell in the glass — like rain.

CLOUDS

Clouds are made of billions of tiny drops of water or ice, which are so light they float on rising air currents (streams of air). Clouds are created when warm, moist air rises and cools. There are many different types of cloud. For example, there are high clouds such as cirrus, mid-level clouds such as altocumulus, and low clouds, such as stratus.

Seeing cirrus clouds means storms or rain might be coming. Cirrus means "curl of hair."

Above 19,500 feet

6,500-19,500 feet

Altocumulus clouds are mid-level clouds that look like cotton balls.

On fine days, you see cumulus clouds.

Up to 6,500 feet

Thick gray stratus clouds make the sky dull and gray and often give rain.

Different types of clouds can help you tell what type of weather is coming.

If you see cumulonimbus clouds, a thunderstorm is on its way.

MAKE A CLOUD

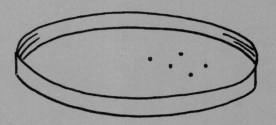

You need:
A can lid
Fine-grained salt
An adult helper

You need to do this in a hot and steamy bathroom. Put the grains of salt on the can lid. Leave for a few minutes. The grains will turn into droplets as water condenses on the salt— just like in a cloud.

QUICK FACTS

Clouds form different shapes depending on how high they are, how fast the wind is blowing, and the amount of moisture in the air.

WHY IT RAINS

All the water that collects in clouds will eventually fall as rain, sleet, snow, or hail. The tiny water droplets or ice crystals that clouds are made of are kept up by rising air currents. As the droplets move around inside a cloud, they bump into each other and combine to make bigger ones. They get so big that they are too heavy to stay in the air, and they fall as rain. If snow crystals or hailstones melt on the way down, they also become raindrops.

QUICK FACTS

Rain is made from tiny water droplets that bump together inside a cloud and form raindrops.

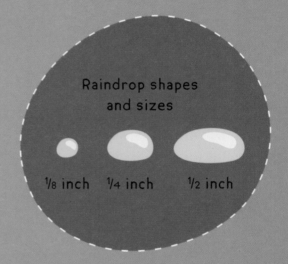

Raindrop shapes and sizes

⅛ inch ¼ inch ½ inch

RAINFALL PATTERNS

Rain does not fall in the same amounts over Earth. Some places, such as the Tropics, have high rainfall and flooding, while others, such as deserts, are so dry there is little rain from one year to the next. Sometimes you find places with high rainfall just a few miles from a dry spot. For example, it can be raining on one side of a mountain but not on the other.

The droplets of moisture that make up a raincloud fall as rain.

Ice crystals usually melt and form raindrops, but if it's really cold near the ground, they fall as snow.

At the top of the cloud are ice crystals.

Water droplets

Ice crystal

At the bottom of the cloud are water droplets only. They combine to form raindrops.

A rainbow forms as sunlight shines through raindrops and is reflected out again.

When raindrops become heavy, they fall as rain.

SNOW, SLEET, HAIL, AND FROST

Snowflakes form when moisture freezes into ice crystals in clouds. As ice crystals bump together, they combine and get bigger. Eventually, they grow so heavy that they fall to the ground as snow. Sleet is snow that melts as it falls. Hail is frozen rain that falls in solid pellets or balls. Frost is ice that forms on the ground when water vapor turns from a gas into a liquid and freezes on cold surfaces.

Frost forms at ground level, especially on clear winter nights.

Villages, towns, and cities can be covered by snow during a blizzard — a snowstorm.

If power lines are damaged, electricity to homes is cut off.

Trees can snap under the weight of snow.

Snow and ice block roads. The snowdrifts can bury cars.

CHAMPION HAIL

Most hailstones are the size of peas, but some can be as big as tennis balls, and the very largest are the size of grapefruits! The largest hailstone ever recorded fell in South Dakota, in 2010. It was 8 inches across and weighed 2 pounds. You wouldn't want to be underneath when this whopper crashed to the ground!

QUICK FACTS

Ice can form snowflakes, hailstones and sleet in the air, and frost on the ground.

HIGHS, LOWS, AND FRONTS

Rising and sinking air produces areas with different air pressure. Where air rises, it creates an area of "low" pressure. As the moist air rises, it expands and cools, producing clouds and rain. Lows often bring stormy weather. Where air sinks, it creates an area of "high" pressure. The sinking air is squashed and it warms, stopping rainclouds from forming. So highs often bring clear skies and sunny weather. Weather "fronts" are the borders between warm and cold air.

In a warm front, a mass of warm air slides above cold air.

Very occasionally, high pressure can be the cause of some very strange weather, such as raining frogs. For example, a tornado called a waterspout can form over water during a high pressure system, before a thunderstorm. The tornado picks up the frogs from the water and then drops them in another place along with rain — so it seems like it's raining frogs!

In a cold front, a mass of cold air moves under warm air.

The moisture condenses (turns back into water), bringing rain and drizzle.

MAKE A LOW

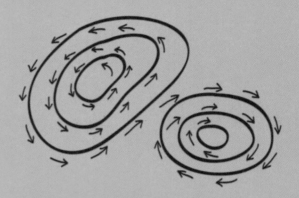

You need:

Half a cup of tea made with tea leaves

A teaspoon

The air surrounding highs and lows spirals around like water swirling round a plughole. You can create a similar effect using a cup of tea with tea leaves at the bottom. Stir the tea with a spoon. The tea leaves that collect at the center are like air moving inward and upward in a low-pressure system.

QUICK FACTS

Different air pressures and temperatures cause different types of weather.

THUNDER AND LIGHTNING

An average of 45,000 thunderstorms strike somewhere on Earth each day! How do thunderstorms happen? Inside huge clouds, water droplets, hail, and ice crystals rub together. This produces a spark of electricity that leaps from the cloud to the ground—that's when you see a flash of lightning. As lightning moves, it heats the air, making it expand very rapidly. This sets up a shock wave, and boom! We hear thunder.

QUICK FACTS

Thunder and lightning happen when electricity builds up inside a cloud.

MAKE STATIC ELECTRICITY

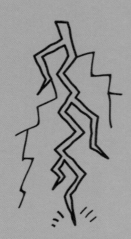

You need:

An inflated balloon

A very thin plastic bag

A dish towel

An adult helper

1. Cut a 1-inch strip from the middle of the bag to make a hoop.
2. Put the hoop on a table and stroke it with the dish towel.
3. Rub the balloon on your hair.
4. Place the hoop above the balloon — the hoop will float! The hoop and balloon are electrically charged and push each other away. The same type of electricity occurs when lightning leaps from a cloud.

Lightning and thunder happen at the same time, but you see the lightning before you hear the thunder. This is because light travels faster than sound.

Lightning can leap from cloud to cloud as well as from a cloud to the ground.

A powerful electric spark leaps from the cloud to the ground — lightning.

HURRICANES

A hurricane is an enormous spinning storm up to 620 miles wide. From space, it looks like a giant wheel of cloud speeding across Earth's surface. Hurricanes form over tropical oceans in summer and fall, where the water is warm and the air moist. They begin as a cluster of thunderstorms. Warm air rises quickly and causes low pressure. The storm spins faster around this low pressure as more air rises and water changes from vapour to liquid (heavy rain). This releases heat, making the storm spin even more powerfully.

QUICK FACTS

Hurricanes are powerful spinning storms that form over tropical oceans in summer and fall.

EYE OF THE STORM

Inside the whirling, swirling hurricane, there is a calm center called the "eye." But around this swirl the most powerful winds that blow at up to 155 miles per hour — as fast as the highest-speed trains.

Hurricanes begin
as thunderstorms.

A hurricane forms over the
ocean and moves at speed over
the water until it slams into the
land, causing great damage.

Heavy rain falls. It releases
heat and fuels the storm.

Light winds around
the hurricane allow
it to grow.

Air expands and cools
as it rises, causing
condensation and
clouds to form.

Warm air rises rapidly upward.

Winds swirl
around the eye
of the storm.

When the hurricane approaches
land, the winds create an area
of low pressure and suck up
a mass of water called
a storm surge.

The heavy rain causes
flooding and the violent
winds destroy buildings,
power lines, and trees.

TORNADOES

A tornado is another spinning storm. It is around 1 mile wide and lasts only a few minutes. Yet the winds inside a tornado are ferocious. Whirling at up to 300 miles per hour, they're the fastest winds on Earth. Tornadoes form over land, below powerful thunderstorms called supercells. Warm air rushing upward starts to spiral and a spinning funnel of air appears below the cloud and reaches down like an elephant's trunk. When it hits the ground, it becomes a tornado.

Tornadoes form below thunderstorms when winds start to spiral upward.

A dark funnel of air forms below the clouds.

This center of very low pressure exerts a sucking force.

The tornado leaves a trail of destruction in its wake.

STAY SAFE

Tornadoes are incredibly powerful and can destroy entire neighborhoods. Think about your own home. Would it survive a fierce storm? Imagine that you are an architect in a country that has tornadoes. Think of ways to protect homes from strong winds. Then go online to find out how architects design such buildings. Are they similar to your ideas?

A whirling tornado lasts only a short while but causes huge damage.

The whirling air creates a tremendous sucking force, like a giant vacuum cleaner. Cars, trucks, boats, and sheds are pulled into the air and hurled around like toys.

QUICK FACTS

Tornadoes are powerful spinning storms that form over land, when warm air beneath a thunderstorm spirals upward.

DROUGHTS AND FLOODS

A drought is an unusually long period of dry weather that can cause a lot of harm. Rivers and lakes dry up, and crops and animals die. Other parts of the world have the opposite problem—they have flooding from rivers and the oceans, and flash floods. These are just as destructive.

When a drought happens, it brings desert-like conditions. It destroys habitats and kills plants and animals.

People are rescued by boat.

Forest fires start in very dry conditions.

Water supplies run out.

Barns are empty of grain and farm machinery is unused.

Crops die because of lack of water.

The soil is cracked and dry.

A cloudburst in the mountains far upstream causes a flash flood.

People may climb on to the roofs of houses to avoid danger.

The river bursts its banks.

Heavy rain in a narrow mountain valley can cause flash flooding and serious damage to people's homes.

DESERTS

Picture a desert. The chances are you think of a hot, sandy place. Deserts such as the Sahara in Africa are indeed scorching hot by day but they are extremely cold at night because there are no clouds to keep in the heat. Some deserts are bitterly cold by day, too. Most deserts are rocky or stony— not sandy at all. All deserts are ultra-dry places that receive less than 10 inches of rain a year.

QUICK FACTS

Droughts happen when not enough rain falls. Floods happen when too much rain falls too quickly.

SATELLITES

How do weather forecasters know it's going to rain? They use spacecraft called satellites high above Earth to study the weather. The satellites have cameras that can photograph clouds and track storms and hurricanes. This helps scientists to work out where storms will strike, so local people can be warned. Some satellites have cameras that can detect heat. They also record temperatures and humidity (the amount of water vapor in the air).

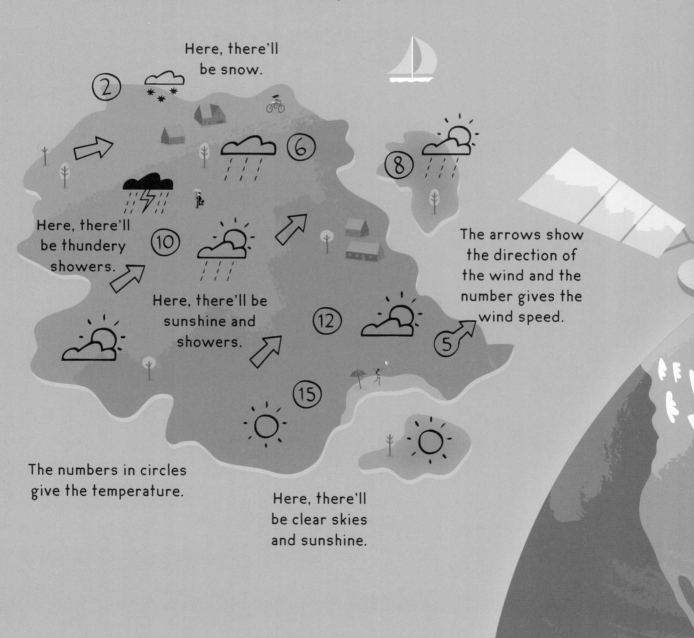

Here, there'll be snow.

The arrows show the direction of the wind and the number gives the wind speed.

Here, there'll be thundery showers.

Here, there'll be sunshine and showers.

The numbers in circles give the temperature.

Here, there'll be clear skies and sunshine.

Information about the weather is collected and fed into computers, which make predictions that are presented as a weather forecast.

LIVE SATELLITE IMAGES

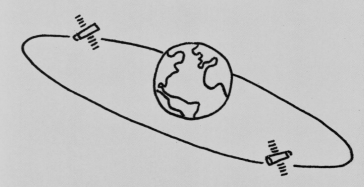

Orbiting satellites send information about the weather back to Earth.

Pick a country in a different part of the world. Go online and search for live weather satellite pictures, plus the name of your chosen country. Take a look at the weather. How is it different to your country? Ask an adult to help you. Are there any similarities? How would your life be different if you lived in that climate?

Scientists can see if a hurricane is forming.

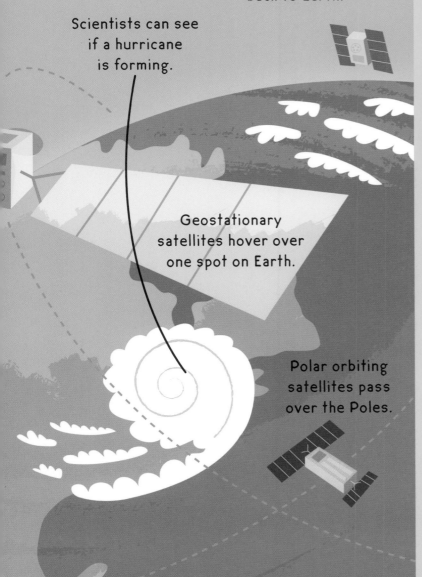

Geostationary satellites hover over one spot on Earth.

Polar orbiting satellites pass over the Poles.

QUICK FACTS

Satellites are electronic devices with cameras and computers, high above Earth. They can help us study the weather.

STUDYING THE WEATHER

Meteorology is the study of weather, and the people who study it are called meteorologists. Although hi-tech equipment is used, some weather conditions are still measured using older instruments such as thermometers to record temperature, and barometers to show air pressure. Anemometers have little cups that spin in the wind to record wind speeds, while rain gauges record rainfall and snowfall.

An anemometer measures wind speeds.

A solar panel provides power.

A temperature sensor records temperatures.

Scientists check the instruments are working properly.

QUICK FACTS

The study of weather is called meteorology.

Meteorologists study weather conditions at weather stations all around the world. This information can be used to forecast the weather.

A weather balloon measures conditions high in the atmosphere.

MAKE A RAIN GAUGE

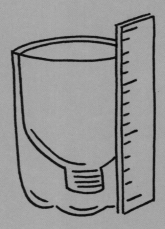

You need:
A plastic bottle
Scissors
A ruler
Tape
An adult helper

You can be a meteorologist, too! Check if rain is forecast for the next week, then try this experiment.

1. Cut the bottle in half.
2. Put the top upside-down in the base to make a funnel.
3. Tape a ruler to the side to measure the rain.
4. Place your rain gauge on the ground outdoors. Check and empty it once a day and record the total rainfall for a week.

CLIMATE CHANGE

Earth's climate changes naturally, but slowly. Gases in the atmosphere, such as carbon dioxide and water vapor, help to keep our planet warm enough for plants and animals to survive. These gases work a bit like the glass in a greenhouse that keeps plants warm, so we call them "greenhouse gases." In the last 150 years or so, pollution from people has added more greenhouse gases to the atmosphere. This has made Earth's climate change quickly in a short amount of time.

Ice covered large areas during the last Ice Age.

LAST ICE AGE —
30% ice coverage

RECENT TIMES —
10% ice coverage

HOW A GREENHOUSE WORKS

You need:

2 thermometers

A glass jar

A timer

An adult helper

1. Place the thermometers in the sunlight for 3 minutes and record their temperatures.
2. Place the jar over one of the thermometers.
3. Check both thermometers every minute for 10 minutes. How did the temperature inside the jar change? The jar traps heat like glass in a greenhouse.

In the past, only natural factors affected Earth's climate, causing gradual changes over time. In today's polluted world, the rate of change is speeding up.

QUICK FACTS

Climate change happens naturally over a long period of time. Pollution has caused climate change to speed up, which is harmful for our planet.

As the last Ice Age ended, the climate warmed and many glaciers melted.

Sea levels rose as melted ice drained into the oceans.

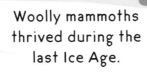

Woolly mammoths thrived during the last Ice Age.

FUTURE WEATHER

The weather looks set to become wilder because of the effects of climate change. Experts believe there will be more extreme rainfall, making floods more common. Dry regions such as Australia, the Middle East, and North Africa could get drier, making it harder for farmers to grow food. As the oceans get warmer, hurricanes could become stronger. Scientists are coming up with ways to slow down climate change.

QUICK FACTS

If we don't work to slow down climate change, the effects of it will damage our Earth.

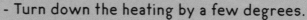

DO YOUR BIT

You can reduce the amount of carbon dioxide your family produces in your home.

- Turn down the heating by a few degrees.
- Switch off lights in rooms with no one in them.
- Turn off computers, TVs, and other devices left on standby.
- Walk or cycle instead of using a car when you can.

If every person does a little, together we can make a big difference.

Alternative forms of energy can help to reduce the effects of climate change.

It might be possible to have solar-powered aircraft.

Growing new forests can help to absorb carbon dioxide.

Wind and solar farms generate clean energy.

Electric trains and cars reduce pollution.

Recycling systems save energy and reduce waste.

Flood barriers guard against rising sea levels.

GLOSSARY

ADAPTED The way that plants, animals, or people are suited to where they live.

AXIS An imaginary line through the center of Earth, on which the planet turns.

CLOUDBURST Sudden heavy rainfall.

CONIFEROUS A type of tree with needle-like leaves and hard cones. Most coniferous trees have leaves that stay on the tree all year — they are called evergreen.

CURRENT The movement of air or water in a particular direction.

DECIDUOUS A type of tree that loses its leaves at the same time each year.

GREENHOUSE GASES Gases, including carbon dioxide and water vapor, that cause Earth's temperature to rise. Some of these gases are produced by humans.

HABITAT The place where a particular type of animal or plant is normally found.

MOISTURE Water vapor present in the air.

SATELLITE A spacecraft that orbits Earth or another planet. It can be used for collecting weather data.

TAIGA A forest biome in which coniferous trees grow.

TEMPERATE Having mild temperatures, which are never very hot or very cold.

TIDES The rising and falling of the sea. Tides are controlled by the moon.

TROPICS The area just above and below the Equator. The climate is warm and hot, and moist all year round.

WATER VAPOR Water in the form of a gas.

WAVES The movement of the sea, most commonly caused by wind blowing over the water.

ANSWERS:

Page 19
Arctic fox — polar
Jaguar — rain forest
Zebra — savannah
Camel — desert